LITTLE LUNCH PRESS

littlelunchpress.com
littlelunchpress@gmail.com

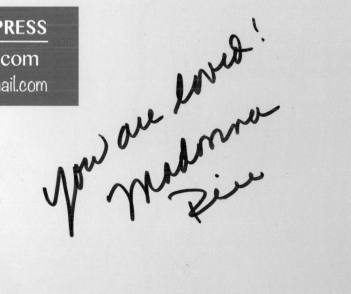

You are loved!
Madonna
Rice

1

MY GRANDMAS ARE AWESOME

Published by
LITTLE LUNCH PRESS
Chicago, Illinois 60655

WEBSITE
www.littlelunchpress.com

ISBN #978-0-692-61910-0

© 2016 LITTLE LUNCH PRESS

Illustration © 2016 LITTLE LUNCH PRESS

Design and Print Services by Pelegan Inc.

Printed in the United States of America
First Edition 2016

Thank you to Raye Ann Saunoris and Pelegan Inc. for their creative ideas.

About this book

"My Grandmas are Awesome"
is a celebration of grandmas and the special
bond they share with their grandchildren.

It encourages readers to cherish and
embrace the love and legacy passed down
from generation to generation.

Told through the eyes of the author's
then five year old daughter, Eileen, this
story expresses a child's deep love for her
grandmas and the special connection and
experiences they shared.

This book is suitable for all age levels,
both children and adults can enjoy it alone
or together. It may spark a conversation to
share a special memory that will enhance
the connection between generations,
or at the very least, make a new memory.

To Rick,

Love, M

My Grandmas Are Awesome!

I'm So Lucky!

I have two Awesome Grandmas.

Their names are
Grandma Mac and Grandma Rice.

Grandma Mac
loves math.
She worked
at a bank.

Grandma Rice enjoys
being a beautician.
She cuts and styles people's hair.

I love when she
brushes my hair.

In the summer, my
brothers and I like to jump
off the front of our boat
into Little Crooked Lake.

This used to make Grandma
Mac very nervous.

But on her 70th birthday,
we all jumped off together!

We play cards with Grandma Mac.

She teaches us lessons
about winning and losing.

12

Grandma Rice used to be afraid of flying in an airplane.

LITTLE LUNCH AIRLINE

But now, she flies to
really fun places.

Sometimes my grandmas call my brothers by the wrong names.

Brendan

Colin

Kevin

Colin

But it's OK,
we know who
they mean.

I
LOVE
my grandmas!

They
are
Awesome!

15

Sometimes
grandmas are
all different, just like
my friends.

My friends love
their grandmas, too!

Jodedah

17

Abby and Tommy's
Grandma Cheri likes
to ride her bike.

It's not very fancy,
but she likes it.

Sometimes, they go on
bike rides together.

Andrew and Michael's Grandma has
always enjoyed reading
to them,
but now
she is blind.

They like to
read to her now,
or she listens to
audio books.

Cal, Declan and Amelia call their grandma, Busia.
It means grandma in Polish. She likes to practice
yoga with her friends. Sometimes she
teaches her grandkids yoga, too!

Morgan's Grandma Colleen likes to cut pretty paper into different shapes.

She makes the cut-outs into homemade birthday cards using different shapes and colors.

Taylor's
Grandma Pam
loves to garden.
Her grandma
grows flowers
and yummy
vegetables.

Taylor helps her pull weeds and
move her flower pots around.

Sometimes, we pick
her flowers as a surprise
for my mommy!

23

Reid's Grandma Sandy likes to run.

She can jog six miles.
It may take awhile, but she is proud of herself.

Vivian and Jade's Grandma Diane enjoys being their
Girl Scout Troop leader. They camp under
the stars and talk late into the night.

But there is something all

GRANDMAS

have in common.

They all
LOVE ♥
their grandchildren
very, very much!

About the Author

Madonna Rice is a first-time children's author. She attended Elmhurst College and received a BS in nursing and psychology. In May of 2016, she graduated from The Institute of Lay Formation in The Lay Leadership Program of University of Saint Mary of the Lake. Madonna has volunteered extensively at Queen of Martyrs, St. John Fisher and Brother Rice High School, in the Chicagoland area.

Presently, Madonna dedicates her time to Marist High School, and is a presenter for the LIVE LIKE YOU ARE PRICELESS® workshops. The workshops were created to empower girls and women to realize their self-worth. She loves writing for children and is happy to share her insights and life experiences. The author lives in Chicago and is the mother of Kevin, Brendan, Colin and Eileen.

About the Illustrator

Raye Ann Saunoris illustrated the award-winning children's book, "The Secret Drawer." Raye Ann is the founder of A Raye of Color, a mural and design business in the Chicagoland area. For many years, the artist taught preschool, including The Farm and Nature Preschool in Palos Park. Raye Ann is married and has two teenage boys, Beau and Bladen, who love their grandmas, too!

Surviving the loss of her firstborn son and daughter, she helps facilitate a Grief Share Group at Trinity Lutheran Church and School in Tinley Park. Raye Ann is dedicated to supporting disabled children and adults through Blue Cap in Blue Island and wholeheartedly embraces everyone through various art forms.

Hi! I am Eileen!

This is a drawing that I made of my
Awesome Grandmas and me...

Do you have an AWESOME GRANDMA too?
"or maybe you have a very
SPECIAL SOMEONE who is AWESOME? "

If you would like, you can draw a
picture and put it in the pocket above!